A GIFT FROM HEAVEN

by

David Steen

SAMUEL FRENCH

FOUNDED 1830

New York   Hollywood   London   Toronto

IMPORTANT BILLING AND CREDIT REQUIREMENTS

A GIFT FROM HEAVEN was originally produced by David Steen and Jim Holmes at The Chamber Theatre in Studio City, California, June 10, 1988. It was directed by Jim Holmes; the set design was by Scot Wood; the lighting design was by Chris Roberts; the sound design was by Mark Webster; the costume design was by Kathy Kish. The stage manager was Patrick Johnston. The original score was composed by Charles Neuschwanger. The cast in order of appearance, was as follows:

MESSY..........Banks Harper
MA SAMUALS...Sarah Hunley
CHARLIE.........David Steen
ANNA...........Leanne Griffin

Also appearing in the extended run were: Beth Grant (Ma); Pat Cochran (Charlie); Jillian McWhirter, Megan Blake (Anna)

CHARACTERS

MESSY, early 20's, wild, unloved daughter of Ma Samuals.
MA SAMUALS, mid-30's, crazed, confused mother of Charlie and Messy.
CHARLIE, early 20's, Ma's reticent son, who yearns to break away.
ANNA, late teens, a shy, disarming, visiting cousin.

SETTING

Rural hills of North Carolina.

THE TIME

Summer, 1954.

ACT ONE
Scene One - Morning
Scene Two - Later that afternoon

ACT TWO
Scene One - The next morning.
Scene Two - Later that afternoon.
Scene Three - Short time later.
Scene Four - Early the next morning.

For
My Family,
and My Buddy, Jim.

ACT I

(Summer, 1954. Morning. We are in the dining room of an old decaying one bedroom shack way back in the hills of North Carolina. It is kept neat, but age and weather have taken their toll. Up against the right wall is an old wood stove used for cooking and heat and a doorway which leads to the pantry and the back porch. Up against the back wall to the right is a curtained off section considered to be MESSY'S bedroom. A doorway leading to MA'S bedroom is in the center of the back wall. Off to the left of the doorway is a picture of Jesus Christ hanging on the wall. Underneath the picture is a crudely built altar with a worn out Bible, a small bottle of holy water, and an assortment of trinkets scattered all about. Along the left wall next to the front door is a heavy tattered rope hanging from a nail. In the center of the room is a dining table with three chairs. Sticking out from underneath the dining table is a pair of feet, toes wrapped around a table leg. The table cloth covers the rest of the body. Off to the side on the floor is a piece of cornbread. MESSY ENTERS from MA'S bedroom. She is humming an old country tune and carries a broom. She walks over to the stove area and looks inside the empty bread tin for her piece of cornbread.)

MESSY. Where's my piece of cornbread?

(A hand reaches out from underneath the table and grabs the cornbread off of the floor. She slams the bread tin down, disgusted.)

MESSY. I bet them damn rats come and get it. *(Starts sweeping.)* How long you gonna work on that? I coulda had it fixed by now. You better get it done before cousin Anna shows up or Ma's gonna tear into you. And if she tears into you it ain't two minutes before she tears into me. And I ain't up for bein tore into today, so you better hustle up and get it done. If you weren't so slow you could maybe get you one of them payin' jobs. Have yourself some money. That's what a man's s'pose to do. Raise some money and bring it home instead of standin' around pickin' his butt relyin' on women to get him through. You remember that Hurly Turner? Boy that sat behind you in the school house. One that used to spit in your hair. Well, he done got hisself a payin' job, done bought him a horse. He's gonna make somethin' of hisself, probably end up in the city. Marry him some pretty gal. If you was smart that's what you'd do. But you's just content to hang around here and get nothin' done. A knot on a log, that's what you are. *(Beat)* I wonder what causes a log to get a knot on it? You got any idea? *(She hits the table with the broom.)* Is your head stuck or somethin'? Why ain't you talked to me?

(MA SAMUALS ENTERS through the front door carrying a bag of vegetables and a jar of white powder.)

MA. What's goin' on in here?
MESSY. *(Covers)* Nothin', I's just singin'.
MA. Where's Charlie?

MESSY. Under there. His heads stuck or somethin'.

(MA takes an ear out corn out of the bag and heads towards the dining table with MESSY right behind her.)

MA. Pity, pity, pity.
MESSY. Pity what?

(MA holds the corn under the table.)

MA. Looky here what I brung ya. It's corn, fresh picked.
MESSY. Why you sayin' pity for?

(MA heads back over to the stove area.)

MA. Old widow Yancy's nearin' her last leg.
MESSY. How do you know?
MA. I can just feel it. She just sits in that rocker starin' out like an old hootie owl.
MESSY. Where'd you get them vegetables?
MA. I's thinkin' about sendin' you over there to spend a couple of days. Help her tidy up her place.
MESSY. I ain't goin' over there.
MA. I heard she's got her a nephew owns a candy store in Willow Springs. You'd be up to your neck in Milk Duds if you was to take up with someone like him.
MESSY. I don't care. I ain't ever goin' back there again.
MA. Why's that?
MESSY. Cause she's full on crazy and I don't want it rubbin' off on me.
MA. She slip her drawers off and toss 'em at you again?

MESSY. No, it was worse than that. Makes me shiver just thinkin' about it.

MA. What'd she do that caused you to shiver?

MESSY. She had me climb up on a chair and drag an old dusty hat box off of the shelf. Said she had some tap dancin' shoes in there.

MA. Tap dancin' shoes? I never know'd her to be a tapper. She can't hardly walk much less tap with them big ol' feet of hers.

MESSY. Worse off, there weren't no tap dancin' shoes in there anyway. Weren't nothin' in there but an old human head.

MA. Human head? What on earth do you mean?

MESSY. A skull's what I mean. I screamed and dropped the box right there. And the skull popped out and the jaw come loose and teeth scattered everywhere. And then she tore into me for droppin' that head. I done had it, I have.

MA. Well, don't get her all riled up. She's liable to kick us outa here and then where would we go?

MESSY. We could figger out somethin'. Closer to town's where we oughta be.

MA. I ain't goin' no closer to town.

MESSY. Why not?

MA. Cause I don't want no people gettin' into our business.

MESSY. Ain't nobody gonna get in our business.

MA. Did you say you were sorry for droppin' that head?

MESSY. No, I just run'd out the door fast as I could.

MA. And left them teeth scattered everywhere? I'm sure I'm gonna hear about that. Lord, you don't do nothin' but kick up trouble ever day of your life. I wish I'd a known before takin' you in. I'd a thought deeper 'bout doin' it.

MESSY. You don't mean that.

MA. Oh, yes, I do. *(MA walks to her altar and picks up a tiny porcelain dish filled with religious dust.)* Come over here and let me sprinkle some Jesus dust in your hair.

MESSY. I don't want none a that dust in my hair.

(MA follows MESSY around tossing dust at her.)

MA. Lemme put some on you feet, so's it might could work itself up.

(MA tosses some dust at MESSY feet. MESSY jumps away.)

MESSY. That hocus-pocus don't do nothin' for me.

MA. It ain't hocus-pocus. It's God's way of workin'.

MESSY. Quit it.

MA. I ought to wet you down and cover you with leaves. That might cure the wildness outa you.

MESSY. I ain't wild. Quit sayin' that.

MA. Leaves mixed with bird's nest for six hours or more.

MESSY. Stop that nonsense talkin', ya hear.

MA. I'm surprised lightenin' and thunder ain't shootin' outa your ears talkin' 'bout God like that.

MESSY. Dang. Here, take a swig of cure-all, so's to calm you down a bit.

(She hands MA the cure-all. MA takes a couple swigs and swishes it around in her mouth before swallowing. She licks her lips.)

MA. She say whose head it was?

MESSY. Huh?

MA. In that old hat box? She say whose head that might be in there?

MESSY. No. She just smirked and rolled her eyes around. Said they washed up on the river bank a long time go. She's got the ribs and leg bones in a box under her bed. I'm done with her. It ain't worth it for two potatoes and a carrot.

MA. She's got her some chickens and she gives us them eggs. You got four eggs for tomorrow, didn't ya?

MESSY. *(Realizes she forgot the eggs.)* Uhhh...

MA. We got company comin' we got to feed. *(Hands MESSY a pan.)* Here, run out back and get some water, so I can make this soup up. We gotta have some hot food ready when cousin Anna gets here. We don't want her sayin we ain't much for puttin it on when cousins come passin through. Go on, git.

(MESSY EXITS. MA starts chopping the vegetables while talking to CHARLIE who is still under the table.)

MA. I don't see how the widow gets her garden to grow and we can hardly get nothin'. I s'pect it has somethin' to do with the ground soil over there. Her's is much darker than that dusty old stuff we got out back. Got to many rocks in it, don't it? Roots ain't got nothin' to hold on to.

(MESSY hurries back inside with the pan full of water.)

MESSY. I been workin' hard today.

MA. You got somethin' done?

MESSY. Uh-huh, I swept up your room and kilt all them spider webs.

MA. Did you tend to that hornets nest out back in the outhouse?

MESSY. What hornets nest?

MA. The one high up in the corner.

MESSY. Them ain't hornets. Them's dirt dobbers.

MA. I don't care what they's called. I want 'em outa there. I can't do my business when they's a bunch of 'em buzzin' around my head. You go on and laugh. I hope you get stung'd the next time you go out there.

(MA puts the chopped vegetables into the pot and takes the jar of powder over to the cabinet. She bends down and opens the cabinet and smells a rotten odor coming from inside.)

MA. Smells like somethin's dead in here. *(She squats down and sees a dead rat stuck in a hole.)* It's another rat.

(MESSY squats down next to MA and looks.)

MESSY. Where?

MA. Right there behind that box. He's halfway in and halfway out. See his tail?

MESSY. Looks like he got stuck.

MA. He done ate that poison I put in there. Lookit that, kilt him 'fore he could git back out.

MESSY. That stuff's quick, ain't it?

MA. Get a stick and poke him out the other side.

(MESSY picks up the jar of powder.)

MESSY. What's this?

MA. Digestion powder.

MESSY. What's it for?

MA. Cleans your inerds out.

MESSY. You gonna take it?

MA. Not till you get them hornets outa the outhouse. Go on and get a stick and poke that rat on out.

(MESSY EXITS. MA continues to cut up vegetables while talking to CHARLIE who's still under the table.)

MA. I wish we had some meat to put in here. Be nice to have somethin' chewy in it. *(She glances back at the cabinet for a beat, then shakes her head and continues chopping vegetables.)* You workin' hard, ain't ya? Don't pay no mind to me. We can take us a walk a little later and do our talkin' then. Hurry on with that stick. That smell's about to level me.

(MESSY runs into the room with a stick.)

MESSY. Here.

MA. Don't give it to me. My hands is all full up.

MESSY. I don't wanna do it.

MA. Just give it a little poke on out the other side.

(MESSY squats and takes a few cautious pokes at the rat.)

MESSY. It won't go through. It's all swoll'd up.

MA. Huh?

MESSY. It's all swoll'd up. It's gonna pop.

MA. It ain't gonna pop. Just poke it on through the wall there.

(She gingerly pokes at the rat's swollen body again.)

MESSY. Ewe. Uh-uh, it's gonna pop.

MA. Give me that. *(MA jabs the rat through the hole.)* You can't be scared of some old dead rat. I ain't never seen nothin' like this in my life. I gotta do everything that gets done around here. It ain't enough I gotta put up with that crazy old widow just to get a dollar or two so's we can eat and live here. I gotta put up with you, too. *(She yanks up the table cloth.)* What are you doin' under there? Ain't you ate that cornbread?
　　MESSY. He got my cornbread?
　　MA. Stop it.
　　MESSY. He done stole my cornbread.
　　MA. Leave him alone.
　　MESSY. That's mine.
　　MA. No it's not. I give it to him.
　　MESSY. I's gonna put butter on it and dip it in some honey.
　　MA. Charlie, git out from under there and go git your hatchet and meet me out front.

(CHARLIE EXITS. MA gathers her things to leave.)

　　MESSY. Where you goin'?
　　MA. Widow Yancy's. Gonna cut her up some cookin' wood.
　　MESSY. I wanna go.
　　MA. No. You're stayin' right here.
　　MESSY. Why?
　　MA. You said you didn't wanna go over there.
　　MESSY. I done changed my mind.
　　MA. You got work to do.
　　MESSY. I done did my work.
　　MA. Keep an eye on that soup.
　　MESSY. That's soup's alright.
　　MA. Then get out back and take care of them hornets.

MESSY. I'm gonna follow y'all and see what y'all is doin'.
MA. You ain't goin' nowhere. You gonna stay right here.

(MA EXITS. MESSY looks after them through the window.)

MESSY. *(Softly)* I'm gonna turn into a butterfly and y'all will
never see me.

(MESSY reaches up and touches her heart. Lights fade.)

Scene 2

*(Later that afternoon. CHARLIE kicks at the front door from out-
side. MA comes out of her bedroom adjusting a new dress.)*

MA. Don't kick the door off it's hinges. I'll get it.

*(She opens the door and CHARLIE ENTERS. He is carrying a pail
of water and an arm full of wood. He sets the wood by the
stove and pours the water into the wash basin.)*

MA. Where you been?
CHARLIE. I's takin' a walk.
MA. What kinda walk?
CHARLIE. Just a walkin' walk. I seen Stappy Tucker an he
told me he'd give me fifty cent if'n I'd drag his old heifer back up
his house.
MA. What was you doin' way up there?
CHARLIE. Just wanderin' round.
MA. I told you to stay around here and not to talk to no people.

CHARLIE. I didn't talk to no people, he talked to me first. Told me about his heifer.

MA. What about his old heifer?

CHARLIE. That it got kilt or died or somethin'. He was walkin' it up the hollar and all the sudden it got stiff and leaned up against a tree. Didn't fall down or nothin'.

MA. How's he know it's died?

CHARLIE. I guess he feel'd it's heart or somethin'. Anyways, he told me he'd give me fifty cent if'n I drag it back up his house.

MA. He still owes us a dollar for pickin' them pecan nuts last year.

CHARLIE. Maybe he'll give me that, too.

MA. Don't even sound like it's died to me. Sound like it's scratchin' up against that tree.

CHARLIE. He said it's died alright. Wants me to help him get it outa there 'fore it gets eat up or rots.

MA. Well, you can't do it know.

CHARLIE. Why not?

MA. I want you here to meet your cousin Anna.

CHARLIE. I can meet her later.

MA. I want us all here so's we can meet her together.

CHARLIE. I gotta help him right now or he's gonna find someone else.

MA. I said you ain't goin'. He wouldn't pay you nohow. He'd have you doin' all that work with nothin' to show for it.

CHARLIE. He said he'd give me fifty cent.

MA. Well, he's tellin' you a lie. He told me he'd give us a dollar for pickin' pecan nuts all day long and he ain't give us nothin'. He's tryin' to take advantage of you and I ain't gonna let him.

CHARLIE. I can take care of myself.

MA. You can? Well go on then. *(She grabs the rope and*

taunts him with it. CHARLIE backs way at the sight of the rope.) Go on and do it yourself. Then find you somewhere to sleep tonight and somethin' to eat in the mornin'.

CHARLIE. I's just tryin' to get me some payin' work, so's I can have me some money.

MA. What do you need money for?

CHARLIE. I's thinkin' I might could get me a horse.

MA. A horse? What are you thinkin' you gonna do with a horse?

CHARLIE. I ain't got that far along on it yet.

MA. Well, don't be thinkin' you can just run off and get you a horse. A horse ain't nothin' but trouble. Sydney Moss done got kicked by his horse and ended up with the mind of a two year-old. Besides, I give you everything you need. I told ya we maybe got us an inheritance comin' someday. And if we put on a good show for cousin Anna Aunt Birdie might be passin' some money our way. And then we'd take us a trip to the ocean. That's what you want, ain't it? To see where the river goes. Well, it goes all the way to the ocean and I'm gonna take you to see it. Ain't nobody else gonna do that for you. *(She brushes aside his hair.)* I'm just tryin' to take care of you. Keep you from gettin' took advantage of.

CHARLIE. Why she comin' here?

MA. Oh, she ain't gonna bother you. She's on her way to Virginia to live. It'll be good for Messy to have a friend to play with for a couple of days. Give us some time to be together. *(She starts smoothing down her dress.)* Well.

CHARLIE. Well, what?

MA. Ain't you gonna say nothin' about my new dress I got on? Aunt Birdie give it to me. I told you she thinks the world of us. I been waitin' for a special day to wear it.

(She holds out the dress and starts twirling around.)

CHARLIE. What you doin' now?

MA. Just floatin' around. It happens every time a lady puts on a new dress for the first time. You just want to hold it out and float around, like Cinderella. Would you like to put on your white shirt? We'd look real nice together.

CHARLIE. I don't reckon.

MA. It'd make a real good impression on your cousin Anna. She'd think we was like society folk, dressed up and all.

CHARLIE. I got work to do.

MA. What do you got to do?

CHARLIE. I got to chop the rest of that wood up.

(CHARLIE heads towards the front door.)

MA. You come back here. You got plenty of time to chop that up. I don't know what to think about you. Talkin' 'bout gettin' a horse and Stappy Tucker's dead cow. *(She walks over to her altar.)* Come on over here, so I can take care of you. *(CHARLIE walks over to the altar and kneels down. He bows his head and closes his eyes.)* It's been a while since we done any spiritualizin', ain't it? I think that's what you been needin'. Why you gettin' so restless. You done forgot about your soul, ain't ya? You been so busy doin' chores around here that your spirit's been dryin' all up. Gettin' dusty, ain't it? If you let your spirit dry up you might as well be dead. The devil gets people that ain't got no spirit.

(MA takes a small bottle of "Holy Water" and holds up to the picture of Jesus. She closes her eyes and silently blesses the water. She pours the water on the back of CHARLIE'S head, then picks up the Bible.)

MA. Gimme a number.

(His head still bowed, CHARLIE calls out a number.)

CHARLIE. Five.

(MA snaps the Bible five times. After the fifth time, she thrust the Bible up and it falls open. CHARLIE calls out another number.)

CHARLIE. Seven.

(MA counts seven verses down from the top of the page and pretends to read from the scripture.)

MA. "And the rains came and fell upon their heads and awakened them. And they arose from the shadows and into the light. Spreading the seeds of the Prophets and filling thyself with each ones spirit. Bringing forth love." *(She lifts CHARLIE'S head.)* You're a man of God, Charlie.

(Suddenly, a scream outside disrupts MA'S ritual. CHARLIE EXITS out the back door as MESSY and ANNA hurry inside.)

MA . What're you holler'n about?
MESSY. They's a whole pack of wild, rabid, dogs after me and Anna. Had to climb a tree to get away. They's almost got Anna. I had to pull her up by her hair or they'd a chewed her legs off.
MA. Mercy me.
MESSY. We'd still be up that tree if'n they hadn't whiffed a coon and took off after it.

(ANNA holds out a small box wrapped with twine.)

MA. Oh, my, you look so much like I remember cousin Gertie. Bless her soul. *(She notices the present.)* Oh, Honey, you shouldn't oughta. *(MA opens the box and sees a small change purse. She looks inside.)* Oh, goodie, an empty change purse. I can sure use that. Anna, honey, give me a hug. I'm sure glad you didn't get eat up by no wild rabid dogs.

(MESSY watches with envy as MA hugs ANNA tight.)

MESSY. I 'bout saved her life's what I did.
MA. I'm so sorry about the fire.
MESSY. Anna here was sleep walkin' and that saved her life.
MA. Oh, my, the Lord was surely with you, Honey. Well, I bet you done worked up an appetite on that bus. We'll get you settled in and have us some supper. Messy, show cousin Anna where your room is then help me get up supper.

(MESSY picks up ANNA'S suitcase.)

MESSY. How'd you know Ma's birthday was comin'?

(ANNA whispers in MESSY'S ear.)

MESSY. It's on out back that way. They's some dirt dobbers in there, so don't be slamin' the door. *(ANNA EXITS out the back door.)* I bet she ain't pee'd all day travelin' on that bus like she was.
MA. Bless her heart. All that she's been through. *(Calls out front door window.)* Charlie, git on in here, suppers up.
MESSY. She's a right pretty gal, ain't she?

MA. Yeah, she's pretty enough. Poor thing's all alone. Ain't got no one to love her.

MESSY. She told me she see'd 'em all burnt.

MA. They burnt to death in hell on earth. That's what happens when you marry into an atheist family. We all warned Gertie about marryin' a man that ain't got no religion. One day you're here and the next day your ashes.

MESSY. She went on and did it anyway?

MA. Shore did. Wouldn't listen to no one.

MESSY. She's real hard headed, wadn't she?

MA. Wrong kinda feelin's for the wrong kinda man. Destruction, that's how the Lord deals with them things. *(Notices mud on the back of MESSY'S leg.)* What's all up the back of your leg?

MESSY. Where?

MA. Right there.

MESSY. Mud. I run through a mud hole gettin' away from them dogs.

(MA wets a cloth to clean MESSY'S leg.)

MA. Stand still and let me get it.

MESSY. Did it get all over my dress?

MA. No, your dress is okay. There you go.

MESSY. Thank you.

(MESSY reaches up to hug MA, but MA pulls away.)

MA. That what you're wearin' to the dance tonight?

MESSY. I don't really feel like goin' to no dance tonight.

(MA gets behind MESSY and starts pinning up her hair.)

MA. Maybe we ought to put your hair up high and get it off your face.

MESSY. Please don't make me go tonight. I wanna stay here with you.

MA. Hold still while I fix your hair.

MESSY. Ouch. You're pullin' it.

MA. Well, if you'd stay still I wouldn't pull it. You got nice hair and it should look good for them boys at the dance. Maybe one of 'em will take a liken' to you and y'all can get married.

MESSY. I don't wanna get married to none of them boys.

MA. They's all lookin' for wives at them dances. That's why they go there.

MESSY. I don't need no husband.

MA. Yes, you do.

MESSY. You ain't got one.

(MA spins MESSY around.)

MA. Turn around and let me see. Oh, you're so pretty. They's all gonna be fightin' over you.

MESSY. Maybe Charlie oughta take Anna to that dance instead of me.

MA. He don't care about goin' to no square dance.

MESSY. I bet he'd have fun at one of 'em.

MA. You know Charlie's shy about things like that.

MESSY. That's cause you won't let him go and be on his on.

MA. He don't fit in with them boys over there.

MESSY. How do you know?

MA. Cause I know he ain't like none of them.

MESSY. You just tryin' to get rid of me.

MA. No, I'm not.

MESSY. You just tryin' to marry me off, so I ain't gotta stay here no more.

MA. You're at the age when you're s'pose to get on out there and find yourself a man.

(MESSY grabs the rat poison off of the shelf.)

MESSY. Why don't you just put some of this rat killer in my food, so you won't have to put up with me no more.

(MA grabs the poison and puts it in a drawer.)

MA. Put that down. Don't play with that.

MESSY. Just put it in my food and see if I care.

MA. There's nothin' wrong with gettin' married.

MESSY. Why ain't you tried to marry Charlie off?

MA. He don't wanna get married.

MESSY. Neither do I.

MA. Quit fightin' with me. I know what you're doin', but it ain't gonna work. *(MA backs away, points.)* I know who you are.

MESSY. *(Confused)* What?

MA. I ain't gotta say it. I know.

MESSY. Why do you act so different to me? *(MESSY reaches up to her heart.)* My chest hurts, Ma. You better hug me.

(MESSY walks over and MA hugs her. MESSY tries to hold on, but MA pulls away.)

MA. Now, you need to show Anna a good time and take her mind off the fire. She can't be sittin' around here doin' nothin'.

MESSY. Maybe she's tired travelin' all day on that bus.

MA. She ain't tired. Girls your age never get tired.

MESSY. I feel kinda tired.

MA. Well, here, take some of widow Yancy's "cure-all" and it'll pep you right up. Take a couple of good swigs for energy.

(MESSY drinks from the bottle and shivers from the taste. MA takes a big swig.)

MA. Good. *(Takes another little swig.)* Now help me get up supper.

(ANNA RETURNS.)

MA. Anna, Honey, you sit right here. I bet you done run up a appetite travelin' all day long. *(MA yells out the window.)* Charlie Samuals, git on in here.

MESSY. I don't know why you yellin' for. He ain't gonna come with her sittin' there.

MA. Lord, I coulda probably been an opry singer if I hadn't ruined my vocal cords yellin' after Charlie. Y'all go on and start passin' things. We ain't gonna wait till winter to nourish ourselves. I'm sure when he smells this soup he'll come a hoppin'. *(MA picks up the bread.)* Messy, pass this to Anna. Anna, that's a musical name, ain't it? *(Sings)* Anna'm walkin' the path to glory, the path I never seen before.

MESSY. Mama.

MA. What? Anna likes my singin', don't ya, Anna? Messy, you bless the food here so's we can get to eatin'.

(They bow their heads.)

MESSY. Lord bless this food we gonna eat.

MA. Amen. Well, you gonna just sit there or are you gonna talk.

ANNA. Umm —

MA. *(Cuts her off.)* Your cousin Letha was a talker. I swear you, well, I don't really swear, but the four years we shared quarters together I had to hang up side down by my legs like a bat and scare her off just to get some sleep.

MESSY. Mama.

MA. Well, it's true. Hang there just like a bat.

(The curtain on the front door is pushed aside. The girls notice. MA turns and sees CHARLIE peeking inside.)

MA. Well, what are you starin' at? Ain't you ever seen people eat before? I told you he'd come a hoppin'.

(The curtain closes.)

MESSY. He's gone.

MA. What? Well, where'd he go?

MESSY. He seen Anna and it probably scared him off.

MA. Messy.

MESSY. I don't mean you's dog ugly, it's just Charlie's weird as horse shit.

MA. Girl, I'm gonna wash that venom out of your mouth with the lye your grandpa left when he died in your bed.

(MESSY sniffs the air.)

MESSY. Smells like somethin's burnin'.

MA. Oh, Lord, my pecan pie. *(MA runs over and checks the pie.)* No, it's okay. I'm gonna set this out back to cool.

(MA EXITS.)

MESSY. That's a lie about Grandpa leavin' lye in my bed. And I'm thinkin' he didn't even die in there either. So, there.

(The front door opens and CHARLIE steps inside. He stares at ANNA and she stares back.)

MESSY. We see'd you before. We see'd you over there. This here's your cousin, Anna. *(CHARLIE and ANNA continue to stare at each other.)* Don't you both talk at once'd.
ANNA. Please'd to meet you.

(CHARLIE just stares.)

MESSY. I told ya he's weird. His ears are crooked.

(CHARLIE walks over and sits at the table. ANNA picks up the bread and offers him a piece.)

ANNA. Would you like some bread? *(He takes a piece.)* Would you like some soup? *(She holds out the soup and he scoops some out. She picks up the butter.)* Would you like some butter?
MESSY. What are you a waitress?
ANNA. No, I's just tryin' to be polite.

(MA RETURNS and sees CHARLIE.)

MA. Well, look what the cat dragged in. Have you met your cousin Anna?

CHARLIE. Yes'm.

MESSY. He can talk.

MA. Ain't she pretty? Like a row of daisy's, a row of daisy's at first full bloom. *(CHARLIE pulls a wad of daisies from his pocket.)* Well, Charlie Samuals, what are you doin' with a pocket full of daisies?

MESSY. Now, I see'd it all.

MA. It's like a omen. An omen from the stars.

MESSY. It ain't no omen. It's a bunch of crumpled daisies.

MA. Run out back and check that pie.

MESSY. That pie's alright. You just took it out there.

MA. Go on, git. *(MESSY EXITS.)* Charlie, did you know Messy and Anna will be goin' to the square dance tonight? Oh, my, y'all will have a big time. I s'pect everyone from both sides of the river will be there. It'll sure be somethin' to talk about.

ANNA. Messy says they usually last up till late in the night.

MA. You'll get a full night's worth a fun in. I'm sure Messy will see to that.

ANNA. Y'all ever go to the dances?

MA. No, me and Charlie are liken' to peacefulness. We like to stay around here where it's peaceful and quite. Don't we Charlie? *(She touches CHARLIE'S face and he hurries away.)* Where you goin'? I got pecan pie comin'. That boy, he's always up and goin'.

ANNA. Hope I didn't scare him off.

MA. No, he's just shy around people. Been that way all of his life. Messy. Bring some pecan pie in here for your cousin Anna. Lord, it's been a long day. I feel like I had a whole day in 'fore lunch.

(MESSY ENTERS with the pie. MA cuts ANNA a piece.)

MESSY. What's got into Charlie?

MA. Here, Anna, have some pecan pie.

MESSY. He come runnin' by me, jumpin' up and down, slappin' hisself like he got a mess a bees in his drawers.

MA. Sit down and quit pryin' into peoples business.

MESSY. I ain't pryin'.

ANNA. This pecan pie's real good.

MA. Well, it should be. I worked half a day on it. But I shouldn't be snappin' at you. I guess I'm just a little tired is all.

ANNA. That's alright.

MA. We don't get many visitors out this far back it seems. Last time I seen most of the family together was at your Uncle Butcher's funeral down in Bennet. I don't believe any your people was there.

ANNA. No, ma'am, I never heard of him.

MESSY. She might a know'd him as Bird Dog.

MA. Messy.

ANNA. How'd he get a name like that?

MESSY. He used to suckle bird dogs and run around with a stick in his mouth.

MA. Stop that. He was born deaf and dumb and had a peculiar sense about him is all.

MESSY. He wore his hair all up like a dog. Had it cut back up his neck real close all the way to his forehead. Then he'd let it grow'd out on the sides real long and narrow like a bird dog's ears.

ANNA. I'da liked to have seen him.

MA. He's passed. Died of old age.

MESSY. He broke his neck tryin' to lick hisself.

MA. That ain't true and you know it.

MESSY. His neck was broke I see'd it.

MA. Well, it don't matter now, he's with the Lord. *(MA crosses to window.)* We sure could use a rain. Yeah, a little wet wouldn't hurt. I s'pose the Lord's been happy these last few weeks. He ain't shed no tears to wet the land. When it's dry and dusty like this seem's like we spend all our time bathin' just tryin' to stay fresh. Did you get enough to eat, Honey?

ANNA. Yes, ma'am, everything was real good.

MA. Well, fine. I guess I'm about full up, too. Y'all excuse me while I step on out around back.

(MA grabs a fly swatter on her way out.)

ANNA. Thank you for supper and all your hospitality.

MA. You're family child. Ain't nothin' we don't do for family.

(MA EXITS.)

ANNA. Your Ma's such a nice person.

MESSY. Yeah, well, she's my adopted ma. My real ma died when I was a baby. My pa took to river-boatin' and couldn't take me along, so Ma Samuals took me on. Did they used to pick you up and hold ya, and carry you around?

ANNA. Who?

MESSY. Your ma and pa. *(ANNA nods.)* It's real sad about 'em dyin'.

ANNA. Well, it was for the better.

MESSY. How do you mean?

ANNA. My ma and pa was different. People was always bein' real mean to 'em. Mean to me, too. Didn't like our kind's what they said. That's why they kilt themselves.

MESSY. They kilt themselves?

ANNA. Uh-huh, committed suicide.

MESSY. How you know that?

ANNA. I seen the suicide letter.

MESSY. What'd it say?

ANNA. Somethin' about 'em wantin' to die in a fire cause they's atheists. I don't remember exactly. It burnt up in the fire.

MESSY. When did you see it?

ANNA. I sleep walked through the kitchen and seen it on the table.

MESSY. Why didn't you do nothin'?

ANNA. Cause, I's asleep.

MESSY. Oh. Well, I sure miss my pa. I don't even remember him I was so young when he left.

ANNA. Don't he ever visit ya?

MESSY. No, he's too busy runnin' a riverboat on the Mississippi River.

ANNA. I been on the Mississippi River, have you?

MESSY. No, but I dated me a boy from Mississippi once'd. He fell in love with me and wanted me to marry him. He had a steady job and everything. But he wouldn't let me wear high heels, show my cleavage, or nothin', and that dog don't run 'round here. Anyways, I ain't lookin' to get married.

ANNA. Why not?

MESSY. Cause, I been accepted to the Tawney Lee School of Beauty and Hair.

ANNA. The Tawney Lee School of Beauty and Hair?

MESSY. Uh-huh, it's a famous beauty school. They's got 'em all across'd America. Lots of movie stars got started there.

ANNA. How'd you hear about it?

MESSY. I dated me a beauty supply salesman once'd. He

taught me all about make-up and skin tint. Told me if I ever wanted to go there just use his name and I'd get right in.

ANNA. What's his name?

MESSY. Umm, somethin' like, Boo somethin'. It's a french soundin' name. I got it written down in my diary. *(She pushes back ANNA'S hair.)* You don't seem to have a flair for make-up.

ANNA. I never really had me any make-up.

(CHARLIE ENTERS and walks over to the table and takes a piece of cornbread and walks back out.)

ANNA. He don't talk much, do he?

MESSY. Well, he ain't the sharpest stick on the fence. He's usually out wanderin' around. We don't see him unless he's hungry. *(MESSY notices a tear in her dress.)* Dang, I got me a rip in my dress.

ANNA. That dress is real pretty.

MESSY. Yeah, a boy I go out with give it to me.

ANNA. You got lots of boyfriends, don't ya?

MESSY. Yeah, I always been real pop'lar. But I just been puttin' everything on hold, so's I can stay here and take care of Ma. She wouldn't know how to get along without me. We're just like sisters.

ANNA. Don't Charlie help her out none?

MESSY. Little bit. But I do most things that need to get done. We're kinda hope'n he'll get married someday. You got yourself a steady?

ANNA. No.

MESSY. That's too bad, ain't it? Girl like you oughta have herself a steady. Well, I reckon we should be gettin' ready to go.

(MA RETURNS and turns on the bare light bulb.)

MA. Y'all better hurry along. It's startin' to get dark.

MESSY. We decided against goin'.

MA. Huh?

MESSY. She ain't up to it.

MA. Yes, she is. She's been sittin' all day. *(MA shakes ANNA.)* She just needs her bones shook up, get the blood runnin'. *(MA slaps ANNA.)* Now, you feel better?

ANNA. Yes, ma'am.

MA. I want y'all down that road in a matter of minutes.

(The girls go into MESSY'S bedroom. MA notices CHARLIE'S shadow behind the front door curtain. She grabs him by the hair and pulls him inside.)

MA. What are you doin' standin' out there?

CHARLIE. Nothin'.

MA. You been doin' alot a peekin' lately, ain't ya? Sit down and have you some pie 'fore you wither up and blow away.

CHARLIE. I done lost my hatchet.

MA. It ain't out in the barn?

CHARLIE. I bet Messy went and hid it somewhere.

MA. Well, why don't you ask her before she leaves. Her and Anna will be gone most of the night. It'd be a good night for us to sit on the porch and listen to the crickets sing. *(The girls come out of the bedroom.)* Well, don't y'all look pretty? Anna, what a lovely sweater. Don't they look pretty, Charlie? Well, speak up, Boy. Do you find Anna pretty?

CHARLIE. Ask Messy 'bout my hatchet?

MA. Why don't you ask her yourself?

MESSY. I ain't see'd his rusty ol' hatchet.

(MESSY and ANNA EXIT.)

MA. Y'all have fun. Don't eat to much.

*(As MA puts the dishes away, CHARLIE moves over and looks out
the window after the girls.)*

CHARLIE. Maybe I should go to one of them square dances.
MA. Oh, it wouldn't be no fun for you. All them boys that
used to pick on you would be there and you don't wanna have to
put up with that, do ya? 'Sides you don't wanna go out and leave
me all alone, do ya? If it's dancin' you wanna do we can do it right
here. I can sing and we can dance around the room. Come on,
Charlie

(MA reaches for CHARLIE'S causing him to go under the table.)

CHARLIE. No.
MA. What's wrong with you?
CHARLIE. I don't wanna dance around the room. If I'm
gonna dance, I wanna do it for real, in a square.
MA. I done told you you ain't goin' to no square dance.
CHARLIE. Why not?
MA. Cause I said so, that's why not. *(She pulls CHARLIE out
from under the table.)* What's done got into you?
CHARLIE. Nothin'.
MA. Don't tell me nothin'. I know when my Charlie's not
feelin' good. You ain't been eatin' enough have ya? When I go into
town tomorrow I'll get an order of ham hocks, so's we can fatten
you up. I'll get some cocoa, too, and make you a fudge cake.

CHARLIE. I don't want no fudge cake.

MA. What do you mean you don't want no fudge cake. That's been your favorite since you was a little boy.

CHARLIE. Maybe I'm changin'.

MA. Changin'?

CHARLIE. I done grow'd up if'n you ain't noticed.

MA. Well, of course I noticed, Charlie. But it's been a while since we been close together. You stayin' off in the barn and all.

CHARLIE. I like it in the barn.

MA. You was give to me to be my man. I've taken care of you and protected you and now you're mine, you hear me, mine. I've done all them things for you and you don't even appreciate it.

CHARLIE. *(Softly)* Yes, I do.

MA. Well, you don't show me you love me no more. You won't even dance with me.

CHARLIE. I don't wanna dance.

MA. You just said you wanted to go to the square dance.

CHARLIE. That's different.

MA. No, it ain't. Dancin's dancin'. Here, let me show ya.

(She reaches up and puts her hands on his waist. She starts to sway, back and forth, pulling him closer with each move. She rubs her face against his chest.)

MA. See, you don't need no square to dance. Just close your eyes and you'll start to hear the music. I hear romantic music, lover's music. *(Sings)* "I hear the stars at night, they always make me feel like dancin'." Do you hear it, Charlie? Do you feel it?

(She reaches up and touches CHARLIE's face, then kisses him softly. Lights fade.)

ACT II

(Early the next morning. MA hurries out of her bedroom getting ready to go to town. She's very upbeat this morning. She peeks behind MESSY'S curtain, then starts gathering her things. ANNA slips out from behind MESSY'S curtain.)

MA. Mornin', Anna. Did you have a big time at the dance last night?

ANNA. Yes, ma'am.

MA. Is Messy up?

ANNA. No, ma'am. She's movin' a little slow. Too much dancin', I s'pose.

MA. Too much of somethin', I'm sure. I got to hurry down the road to catch a ride into town. Help yourself to what you need. It's kinda bare, but I'll stock her back up best I can. You don't have an extra dollar, do ya?

ANNA. No, ma'am, I don't.

MA. Don't matter anyway. *(MA hollers out of the window.)* Charlie, don't forget to meet me later down the road with the wagon. Oh, Lordy, hope I have everything. *(Stops at door.)* Anna,

Honey, I's thinkin' you be sure to tell Aunt Birdie how much of a big time we all had together. Will you do that for me? Put in a good word for us out here in the sticks?

ANNA. Yes, ma'am, I will.

MA. Well, idn't that sweet. Gotta get goin'. Bye-bye.

(MA EXITS. MESSY comes dragging in the back door looking a mess. Her dress is ripped and hangs from her shoulder.)

MESSY. I thought she'd never leave.

ANNA. Messy, where you been? I's worried about you.

MESSY. I just been down watchin' the river run by.

ANNA. What happened? Your dress is all ripped up.

MESSY. I musta run into a tree. I can fix it.

(MESSY eases into a chair. ANNA sees a scratch on her face.)

ANNA. Your face is scratched up, too.

MESSY. I said I run'd into a tree. Would you be sweet and hand me that washin' pail?

(ANNA takes the wash basin over and MESSY begins cleaning herself. First her face, then shifting her clothing around she washes her entire body.)

ANNA. You sure you're okay?

MESSY. I musta had a little too much celebratin' punch. That's what Bobby Springer called it. He told me I could dance a little better if I had me some. Must be true cause after I drank a few cup fulls seems everybody wanted to dance with me.

ANNA. Where'd you run off to?

MESSY. Bobby said he had somethin' he wanted to give me. So he took me for a walk down the path that leads to the river. We stopped in a clearin' cause he wanted to dance. We musta been followed cause when we started dancin' someone tapped him on the shoulder tryin' to cut in on the dance. Bobby didn't like it. Said he was gonna do it first. They's almost started fightin', so I told the other boy he could dance with me after Bobby got done. Then I looked around and there was five or six other boys surroundin' me, wantin' to press up against me. I felt sorry for 'em. Lots of them boys ain't never been loved. Them's the ones that hold on real tight, cling to ya.

ANNA. Why did you let them do that to you?

MESSY. They didn't mean to hurt me. They all said they loved me. Look at what I got. *(She pulls out an old pair of earrings.)* Pair of fancy earrings. Ain't they pretty? They's a couple of rhinestones missin', but that's okay.

ANNA. You should tell Ma about it.

MESSY. No. She wouldn't understand. Them boys all needed me.

ANNA. We oughta tell somebody.

MESSY. No. Don't say nothin' to no one. I don't wanna get kicked out and left all alone. My hearts too weak. I need to feel wanted. It keeps my heart strong. If I don't feel wanted my heart will stop beatin'.

ANNA. Who told you that?

MESSY. The doctor. I was real sick and thought I was gonna die. I heard Ma and the doctor talkin' about it. He told her I needed lots of attention to keep my heart strong. That's why she loves me so much and why we need to be together. I can't have her gettin' upset, so please, don't say nothin', alright?

ANNA. Alright, I won't say nothin'.

MESSY. You're so nice, Anna. You could be real pretty, too. *(MESSY looks at her breast and sees a mark on it.)* I believe one a them boys done bit me on the tittie. *(She struggles up from the chair.)* I'm gonna try and get me some sleep.

ANNA. You alright?

MESSY. I feel like I been in a rodeo's all.

ANNA. Here, let me help you.

MESSY. No, I'm alright, really I am.

(She crosses to her bedroom and stops. She touches her ripped and torn dress.)

MESSY. This is a pretty dress, ain't it, Anna?

ANNA. Yeah. It's a real pretty dress.

MESSY. It's worth fixin' up.

(MESSY EXITS into her room. The front door curtain is slightly pushed back as ANNA picks up the wash basin and puts it away. She turns and catches a glimpse of CHARLIE'S face as he lets the curtain go.)

ANNA. Mornin', Charlie.

(CHARLIE answers from outside the door.)

CHARLIE. *(O.S.)* Mornin'.

ANNA. Why don't you come on in?

CHARLIE. *(O.S. Beat.)* Why?

ANNA. So's we can talk better.

(CHARLIE ENTERS stopping just inside the door.)

CHARLIE. How was the dance?

ANNA. We had a real good time. Maybe you oughta come to the next one.

CHARLIE. Yeah, I been meanin' to, but I been to busy.

ANNA. What you been doin'?

CHARLIE. Oh, I been doin' lots of things.

ANNA. Like what?

(He points to the front door.)

CHARLIE. I moved this door from the back to the front. Cause it got windows in it. Lets the breeze come through. It can get hot in here if there ain't a breeze comin' through. The other door ain't got no windows, so we'd leave it stay open, but the rats come through it and start eatin' the food. Ma didn't like it, so I moved 'em around.

ANNA. That was a smart thing to do.

CHARLIE. Yeah, it was kinda smart. *(He walks up next to the dining table.)* I fixed that table, too. *(He suddenly leaps flat footed onto the dining and lands in a squatted position.)* It used to be wobbly, but it ain't no more. I fixed that leg, so it don't wobble no more. Go ahead, try and shake it.

ANNA. Okay.

(ANNA moves over and gives the table a little shake.)

CHARLIE. See, it don't wobble.

ANNA. No, it don't wobble at all. I guess you have been busy fixin' all them things.

(CHARLIE leaps back to the floor.)

CHARLIE. Yeah, they's lots of things to do around here. *(There is a moment of uncomfortable silence before CHARLIE speaks again.)* Do you like to fish?
ANNA. Yeah, I like to fish.
CHARLIE. What do you like better, fishin' or dancin'?
ANNA. Depends. What do you like better?
CHARLIE. Dancin'.
ANNA. Dancin'?
CHARLIE. Yeah, I'm better at fishin' than dancin', but I like dancin'. *(Beat)* I'm goin' fishin' in about a minute.
ANNA. In about a minute?
CHARLIE. Yeah, it only takes me about a minute to get ready to go.
ANNA. Where you gonna go?
CHARLIE. Down at the river.
ANNA. I heard about the river.
CHARLIE. You seen it yet?
ANNA. No.
CHARLIE. It's a pretty river.
ANNA. I'd like to see it.
CHARLIE. Well, I'm gonna be passin' by here in less than a minute. If you're all ready you can foller along.
ANNA. I don't think I can be ready to go in less than a minute.
CHARLIE. Oh. *(He EXITS, but in a moment returns.)* It's gonna take me a little longer than I expected to get ready, so we'll probably be ready about the same time.
ANNA. Okay.
CHARLIE. Since we got some extra time. Maybe you oughta put some food up to bring along for lunch.
ANNA. I could make up a picnic lunch. Is that okay?
CHARLIE. How long's that gonna take?

ANNA. Not long. I just have to see what all we got.

CHARLIE. Yeah, we can have a picnic. I know where they's a rock we can have a picnic at. I'll bring along a stick to keep away the lizards.

ANNA. Okay, I'll get ready.

(CHARLIE hurries out the back door. ANNA gathers food. CHARLIE quickly returns wearing a white shirt under his overalls. He is carrying two small sticks.)

CHARLIE. Ready to go.

ANNA. Yeah. What a nice white shirt.

CHARLIE. I brung a stick for you, too.

(He holds out a stick for ANNA.)

ANNA. Thanks.

(He offers his arm to ANNA. They EXIT. Lights fade.)

Scene 2

(Later that afternoon. Offstage, we hear MA yelling.)

MA. (O.S.) Charlie, Messy, Anna! *(She ENTERS carrying a bag of grocery goods.)* Where is everybody?

(MESSY comes out of her room still half asleep.)

MESSY. What are you hollerin' 'bout?

MA. Where's Charlie? He was s'posed to meet me at the road with the wagon. I had to carry all this stuff up here by myself. Half of it's still down there by the road under a tree. What am I s'posed to do? Go back and forth luggin' all this stuff up here by myself? You want me to have a heart attack? Where's Anna?

MESSY. I don't know.

MA. You don't know nothin', do ya? All you know how to do is lie in bed on your butt all day. What happened to your face?

MESSY. I run'd into a tree.

MA. That's what you get stayin' out all night drinkin' and carryin' on.

MESSY. I wadn't out all night drinkin' and carryin' on.

MA. Don't take me for no fool. I looked in your room and you weren't there. That's a real good impression to set for your cousin Anna. She told me a lie to cover up for you. She been here less than two days and you already got her lyin'. I ain't runnin' no whorehouse here. I ain't gonna put up with a couple of hussies stayin' out all night drinkin' and tellin' lies. I want you to find a nice boy and get married. But you'll never get married if you give it away. Now, get in there and put on some clothes. Then you get over to widow Yancy's, clean her up and put her on some supper. And I don't want you back here till mornin'. *(MA takes the bottle of cure-all out of the drawer and finishes it off and hands it to MESSY.)* Get her to fill this up, too.

(Offstage, we hear laughter. CHARLIE and ANNA ENTER and freeze when they see MA.)

MA. Where you been? You were s'posed to meet me at the road with the wagon. I had to lug all this stuff up here by myself. Nearly give me a heart attack. What you two been doin'?

CHARLIE. Fishin'.

MA. Fishin'? What are you doin' with your white shirt on? I told you not to put that on 'cept for special occasions, or when you and me went to town. Is this some kind of special occasion I don't know nothin' about? Where's the fish? You been fishin', where's the fish?

CHARLIE. We didn't catch none.

MA. You didn't catch none? I never know'd you to go fishin' at the river and not catch a fish.

ANNA. They just weren't bitin'.

MA. I ain't talkin' to you, Anna, you just be. You get all spruced up to go fishin' and you don't catch a fish. The fish ain't bitin', but you stay there all day and forget to meet me at the road with the wagon. Do I have to get the rope again? Do we have to start all over? I want you to stay away from each other, you here me? Now, get that wagon and go down the road and get everything I left under that tree. Then go out back and cut all the rest of that wood and stack it in the barn. And since you ain't done nothin' all day, you probably got no appetite, so you just work on through supper. *(She yanks the shirt off of CHARLIE.)* Now, take off that shirt and don't ever put it on again unless I say so.

(CHARLIE EXITS.)

ANNA. Ma Samuals, please don't take it all out on Charlie. I'm just as much to blame.

MA. Don't tell me how to handle my affairs. Messy, get out here! Y'all done given me a headache. I hope you're happy.

(MA EXITS. MESSY steps out from her bedroom.)

MESSY. Anna, where y'all been?

ANNA. We went fishin' down at the river.

MESSY. He forgot about meetin' Ma and now she's all ticked off.

ANNA. I know. She's real mad, ain't she?

MESSY. Shoot, she lit into me before y'all got home. And I can't get no sleep and I got me a bad hungover.

ANNA. Why'd she lite into you?

MESSY. She know'd I stayed out all night and you lied about it. Then she called us a couple of hussies and said she weren't runnin' no whorehouse here. This place is more like a nuthouse. And I ain't no hussy either. She got a lot of nerve callin' us hussies when she give birth to a nut outa wedlock.

ANNA. Charlie ain't no nut. He's different when he's not around you two.

MESSY. Believe me, I've known lots a boys and none of 'em's as weird as Charlie. 'Cept for maybe Sidney Moss.

ANNA. Who's he?

MESSY. He's a boy got kicked in the head by his horse. *(Points to her head.)* Got a dent right here so deep you could fit a wedge of cheese in it.

ANNA. Well, I been with Charlie all day long and he really was nice to me.

MESSY. Well, he ain't ever been really nice to me. He hardly says nothin' to me at all.

ANNA. He told me you been mad at him cause Ma paid more attention to him than she does to you.

MESSY. That ain't true. She's paid more attention to me and he done got jealous and wouldn't talk to me.

ANNA. He said he don't feel so right bein' around y'all all the time.

MESSY. Then why don't he just up and leave?

ANNA. He told me Ma depends on him to get things done around here.

MESSY. I can do all the things he can do. She just don't want him to feel useless is all. My feelin's is it's way past time for him to get out on his own. Hell, how many times can you move the outhouse around.

ANNA. He knows that.

MESSY. What?

ANNA. That he ought to be out on his own.

MESSY. He does?

ANNA. He told me he would like to get hisself a job, maybe pick up a horse, and move to the city.

MESSY. Charlie said that?

ANNA. He sure did.

MESSY. So, y'all had a good time bein' together today?

ANNA. Uh-huh. It was kinda scary at first, but then it felt alright.

MESSY. What'd it feel like?

ANNA. Well, you're the one oughta know. You've had lots of boyfriends and I ain't had none.

MESSY. I's just testin' ya. Testin' to see if y'all's really got feelin's for each other. Did he put his arms around ya and hold on real tight?

ANNA. No.

MESSY. Why not?

ANNA. I don't know. Maybe he's shy about things like that.

MESSY. How'm I s'pose to tell if you ain't been up close and held on to him?

ANNA. What's it like when a boy holds ya?

MESSY. It's like a warm feelin' at first. Like your body's fill-in' up with hard liquor. But, then, when it's over it feels all empty again. Like wakin' up from a dream and reachin' out to grab what you're dreamin' 'bout but there ain't nothin' there. That's why I keep doin' it. Cause I know one time I'm gonna wake up and it's gonna be there.

ANNA. What's gonna be there?

MESSY. That fulled up feelin'. When that don't go away you know you found what you're lookin' for.

ANNA. I bet that feels good.

MESSY. I bet it do, too. Anytime you get that feelin' you got to grab it and hold on tight, so's it can't be taken away. Like take Charlie, just cause he ain't spit and polished, that's okay, cause some women ain't spit and polished either. And they better catch what's bitin'. Especially when they's young and look worth fertil-izin'. That's when you gotta hook 'em or you might not never get a nibble again. Now you get what I'm talkin' about?

ANNA. Yeah, I'm catchin' on pretty good. Thanks for talkin' to me about them things.

MESSY. Well, if you got anymore questions just give me a holler. I probably know the answers. *(She gets up to leave.)* Damn, I'm sore. If you want somethin' to eat you gonna have to make it yourself. I gotta run on over to the widow's tonight and see she's taken care of. I reckon I'll see you in the mornin'.

ANNA. Alright.

(MESSY takes out a small bottle of perfume and hands it to ANNA, then EXITS. ANNA looks at herself in the mirror by the window. A flash of heat lightening comes through the window. She smells the perfume and puts some on. She takes a piece of cornbread off the stove and EXITS. Lights fade.)

Scene 3

(Short time later. Lights stream through the cracks in the rear stage right wall as it slowly opens to reveal a barn. Heat lightening flashes periodically throughout the scene. Hearing something, CHARLIE has opened the door and is startled by ANNA standing there.)

ANNA. I didn't mean to scare you.

CHARLIE. You didn't scare me.

ANNA. What are you doin'?

CHARLIE. Nothin'.

ANNA. I couldn't sleep cause of all the lightenin' flashin' around.

CHARLIE. That's nothin' to be scared of. It's just heat lightenin'.

ANNA. I brought you some cornbread. I thought you might be hungry after cuttin' all that wood.

CHARLIE. I didn't cut all that wood. She got to ask me nicer if she wants me to cut all that wood. I went over Stappy Tucker's and told him he ought to give us that dollar he owed us.

ANNA. Who's he?

CHARLIE. Man we picked pecans for.

ANNA. Did he give it to ya?

CHARLIE. He didn't want to at first, but I'd carried my hatchet along and that mighta helped.

ANNA. Is that where you stay?

CHARLIE. Yeah. Pretty much it is.

ANNA. Can I come inside there?

(CHARLIE glances back at the cabin, then lets ANNA ENTER.)

CHARLIE. Yeah.

(ANNA steps inside the barn and notices a pad of paper sitting on a bale of hay.)

ANNA. What's that paper there?

(CHARLIE hides the pad behind his back.)

CHARLIE. Nothin'.
ANNA. Wait, Charlie, let me see it.
CHARLIE. Uh-uh.
ANNA. What is it?
CHARLIE. Nothin'.
ANNA. Then let me see it.
CHARLIE. Better not.
ANNA. Is it a diary?
CHARLIE. No, it ain't no diary.
ANNA. I bet it's a diary.
CHARLIE. You wrong about that.
ANNA. Come on, Charlie, I won't tell nobody I seen it.
CHARLIE. It's my writin's.
ANNA. Your writin's?
CHARLIE. Yeah.
ANNA. What kinda writin's?
CHARLIE. Just writin' writin's.
ANNA. What do they say?
CHARLIE. Not much a nothin'.
ANNA. I'd like to see 'em if I could.
CHARLIE. Why?
ANNA. Cause I'm interested in 'em.

CHARLIE. Ain't nobody ever see'd 'em before.
ANNA. Then I can be the first.
CHARLIE. Can you read?
ANNA. I can read pretty good.
CHARLIE. Okay.

(He hands her the pad and they sit on the bale of hay. ANNA stares at the first page, puzzled.)

CHARLIE. Them's just markin's from sharpenin' my pencil.
ANNA. Oh. *(Flips the page.)* Is this it here?
CHARLIE. Yeah, that's the first one I done.
ANNA. *(Reads, slow and flat.)* Rain...rain...rain...Dirt...dirt...dirt
...mud.

(She looks up.)

CHARLIE. S'posed to be funny.
ANNA. Oh, it is funny. I like it. Can I read another one?
CHARLIE. Yeah.

(ANNA flips the page.)

ANNA. *(Reads, slow and flat.)* Stand and chew....swat my tail.
Stand and chew....here comes the pail. Stand and chew....I feel a
hand. Oh, my god, it's the milkman.
CHARLIE. It's about a cow.
ANNA. I know, it's funny, too. How much writin' you done?
CHARLIE. Well, them are some of my early ones. This one
here's my last one.

(He hands her a folded up poem from his pocket.)

ANNA. *(Reads)* Love, it's the smells and memories of whatever it was. It don't matter, if it was love. *(She hands the poem back.)* That was beautiful, Charlie. It made me feel funny all over. I think you're really special.

CHARLIE. How come?

ANNA. You're not like anybody I ever met before.

CHARLIE. I ain't?

ANNA. No. You're nice, and you're smart, and you're real funny, too. I had a nice real time bein' together with you today.

CHARLIE. Did you have lots of friends livin' in Mississippi?

ANNA. No. People didn't like us so much. I spent most of my time alone.

CHARLIE. I feel like we'd a been friends if'n we'd grow'd up together.

ANNA. Me too. I wish I didn't have to leave here tomorrow.

CHARLIE. Me, too.

ANNA. You think you ever wanna see other places besides around here?

CHARLIE. Yeah, me and Ma's s'posed to be takin' a trip pretty soon.

ANNA. Maybe you can come visit me in Virginia someday.

CHARLIE. Yeah, I might could do that.

ANNA. I wish you coulda come to the dance last night. I'd a had more fun if you woulda been there. Where'd you learn to dance? At the dances around here?

CHARLIE. No. I just kinda picked it up.

ANNA. Picked it up, where?

CHARLIE. I just kinda picked it up by myself.

ANNA. By yourself?

CHARLIE. Yeah. I just mainly done it by myself.

ANNA. Alone, with no partner? *(CHARLIE nods.)* Well, that ain't no fun. Here, let's try it together.

(She takes CHARLIE'S hands and pulls him up. She puts his hands on her hips.)

ANNA. Put one hand here and the other one here. *(They start to sway, back and forth.)* See, that's fun, ain't it? I wish we had some music.

CHARLIE. We don't need no music. Just close your eyes and you'll start to hear some music. I hear romantic music, lovers music. Do you hear it Anna? Do you feel it?

(They stop swaying. ANNA reaches up and softly kisses CHARLIE'S face, then she kisses him on the lips. As lights begin to slowly fade there is a Flash of heat lightening. She reaches up and slips his overall straps off his shoulders. His overalls fall to the ground. Another Flash of heat lightening as CHARLIE lifts her dress straps off of her shoulders and her dress falls to the ground. She moves closer to him. He pulls her tight against his body. Another Flash of heat lightening as he lays her down on the blanket covered hay where he sleeps. She pulls him down to her. Another Flash of heat Lightening as the lights fade.)

Scene 4

(Early the next morning. A match strike illuminates MA SAMUALS on her knees before her altar. She lights a candle and raises it into the air. As she mumbles the words to her prayer, she drips wax onto the back of her hand. She waves her wax covered hand slowly back and forth before the altar.)

MA. The devil's skin chills the air. But God's fire stands hot calling mercy its friend. Fear runs and flows like a river, but not past the arms of the Lord.

(As MA douses the flame with her palm, the front door slowly opens and ANNA ENTERS, startled to see MA.)

MA. Mornin', Anna.

ANNA. Mornin'.

MA. I thought you was in there sleepin'.

ANNA. No, ma'am. I wadn't sleepin' so good, so I took me a walk.

MA. I hope you're not upset about yesterday. It's just I's lookin' after Charlie. He don't like bein' around strangers so much. Cause they might up and try to carry him away. The strangers would. It's been that way ever since he was born. I been fightin' for him all my life, tryin' to protect him from evil. You know about religion, child?

ANNA. Little bit.

MA. I ain't talkin' church-house religion. I'm talkin', one on one, messages from God. Charlie knows, cause he's special from heaven. He was give special to me when I was just twelve years old.

ANNA. Someone give him to ya?

MA. My Ma's brother give him to me. He come through here for a short stay after Ma had died off. He had been evangelizin' to the people not too far from here. Right off, he seen somethin' special in me. And he wanted to ritualize me, so's I'd have a part of God in my soul. We took us a walk down by the river where he had dealt with the sinners before. And he took me by the hair and had me kneel down and pray. And he come from behind me and ran river water down my bare back till it run down my legs. And I felt the pain of the devil leavin' as God come into my body. At first it stole my breath away. Caused my fingers to dig in the mud. Then all the sudden it stopped. And I turned to see my Pa had been watchin' us. I tried to stop him, but he pushed me down and dragged Ma's brother away with his horse. The devil people had got him. Just like he said they would.

ANNA. Did you ever see him again?

MA. Not till I had Charlie. They got the same face. *(She goes over to the altar and picks up the Bible and the small bottle of "Holy Water".)* This was his Bible here. Feel how warm it is. *(ANNA touches the Bible.)* I can save you from the devil people. Bow down and kneel to the floor.

(ANNA kneels. Then MA removes ANNA'S dress straps from her shoulders and ANNA covers herself as her dress falls to her waist. She pours the water down ANNA'S bare back the same way MA'S brother had done to her. She runs her hand down ANNA'S back, then notices something in her hair.)

MA. What's this in your hair, Anna?
ANNA. I don't know.
MA. You got somethin' in your hair?

(MA grabs ANNA' hair to get a closer look.)

ANNA. Owww, you're pullin' it.

(MA pulls some hay from ANNA'S hair.)

MA. It's hay ain't it? Was you in the barn?

ANNA. I wadn't doin' nothin'.

MA. Did you see Charlie? *(She grabs ANNA'S hair.)* I smell him all over you.

ANNA. We was just talkin'.

MA. You tryin' to take him from me?

(MA drags ANNA over and throws her into the rocking chair.)

ANNA. You're hurtin' me.

MA. Where you got him? You got him in your belly?

ANNA. I ain't got him.

MA. You tryin' to leave here with Charlie in your belly? *(She spreads ANNA'S legs apart and reaches up her dress.)* Let him out or I'll cut him out myself.

(MA grabs the butcher knife. ANNA screams. The front door bursts open and CHARLIE runs inside.)

CHARLIE. Ma.

(MA sees CHARLIE and drops the knife. She lets go of ANNA. She raises both arms and begins talking in tongues. Her eyes roll back and she falls to her knees and then to the floor passing out.)

CHARLIE . Anna. *(ANNA starts to run away. CHARLIE stops her.)* Wait.

ANNA. She was tryin' to kill me.

CHARLIE. Why?

ANNA. She knows what we done.

(ANNA pulls away from CHARLIE and goes into MESSY'S bedroom. CHARLIE picks up the knife as MESSY ENTERS. She sees MA lying on the floor. She runs to MA'S side.)

MESSY. Oh, no, what happened?

(MESSY cradles MA'S head in her arms.)

CHARLIE. She was goin' after Anna.
MESSY. Ma, you okay? Ma, please wake up.
CHARLIE. She had that knife and she was goin' after Anna.
MESSY. Get some water, Charlie.
CHARLIE. We ain't done nothin' wrong.
MESSY. Go out back and get some water.

(CHARLIE runs out. ANNA comes out with her suitcase.)

MESSY. Anna, what happened?
ANNA. She said I was tryin' to take Charlie away.
MESSY. Hold on a second. It's gonna be alright.
ANNA. I can't stay here no more.
MESSY. No, you don't have to leave.
ANNA. Give this to Charlie, so he'll know where I'll be livin'.

(MA moans, frightening ANNA. She runs out the door.)

MESSY. Anna, wait. Don't go nowhere.

(MESSY goes back to MA'S side. CHARLIE comes back inside and carries the water to MESSY and looks around the room. MESSY takes a wet cloth and starts wiping MA'S forehead with it.)

MESSY. Ma, wake up, it's gonna be okay.
CHARLIE. Where's Anna?
MESSY. I'm here now. You're gonna be just fine.
CHARLIE. Where's Anna?
MESSY. She's gone, Charlie. Ma run her off.

(MA starts waking up. MESSY kneels by her side.)

MESSY. Stay down, Ma. It's gonna be okay.
MA. Where's Charlie?
MESSY. He's right there. Stay down till you get your strength
back.
MA. I always knew they was comin'.
MESSY. There ain't nobody here. Just me and Charlie's here.
MA. Tie up that door. Don't let nobody in.
MESSY. Shhh. Just lie back a minute till you catch your
strength.

(MA lies back down and MESSY continues soothing her.)

MA. Where's he now?
MESSY. He's right over there. Don't worry about him. I'm
gonna take care of you. You're gonna be just fine.

(MA settles down. MESSY looks over to CHARLIE.)

MESSY. It's okay, Charlie. You ought to go find Anna.

(CHARLIE turns to leave.)

MA. Don't you go nowhere. You'll burn up and die.

MESSY. Hush up now. Don't get all excited.

(MESSY tries to hold her down, but MA breaks free.)

MA. Let go of me. *(She grabs CHARLIE.)* Get down on your knees.
MESSY. Ma, stop.

(MA drags him over to the altar.)

MA. We got to start all over again.
MESSY. Please, let him go.

(MA tries to force CHARLIE to his knees.)

MA. Get down on your knees. Now. *(CHARLIE stiffens and doesn't budge.)* Do I have to get the rope?

(MA grabs the rope. MESSY struggles with MA for the rope.)

MESSY. You ain't gonna tie him up no more.
MA. Let go of me.
MESSY. There ain't gonna be no rope no more.

(MESSY jerks the rope out of MA'S hands and throws it into the stove fire. MA begins to softly sing.)

MA. "Precious Lord, who lives within'. Give me strength, till comes the end. Help me fight, away life's sin. Oh Lord, who lives within'."

(MA stands still and alone. MESSY tries to comfort her.)

MESSY. It's okay, Ma. Charlie don't have to leave. Me and him's friends now. We all gonna get along real good. It's gonna be like a family house.

(MA goes to CHARLIE.)

MA. It's time for us to go.
MESSY. Where you goin'? Where you gonna go?
MA. To the ocean. Charlie wants to know where the river goes and I'm gonna show him.
MESSY. That river don't go to no ocean.
MA. I touched it and put it in my mouth. It don't taste like no river. It taste like God's sweat. The ocean is pools of God's sweat he left while building these mountains. That's why Charlie was strong. Cause I drank from the ocean. Now he's got to drink it, so he can get stronger.
MESSY. I wanna go, too.
MA. Get away from me, devil.
MESSY. I ain't no devil.
MA. You can have the house.
MESSY. I don't want this old house.
MA. You can have all them dishes.
MESSY. I need to stay with you. I can't be here alone.

(MA opens the drawer looking for her cure-all.)

MA. Where's my cure-all?
MESSY. Please don't leave me.
MA. Where'd you put my cure-all?

MESSY. I'll be good and do anything you want.
MA. Charlie, go pack up your stuff.

(CHARLIE stands still.)

MESSY. What about my heart? If you leave me here alone my heart will stop beatin'.
MA. No, it won't.
MESSY. Yes, it will. If you don't take care of me my heart'll stop beatin' and I'll die.
MA. That's a lie.
MESSY. I heard the doctor say it. I heard him tell you to love me. He said I was special, too, just like Charlie.
MA. I said go pack up your stuff.
MESSY. Don't Charlie, don't let her leave me. Please, Ma, please take me with you. Please don't leave me alone.

(MA pushes MESSY away.)

MA. I never wanted you in the first place.
MESSY. That's a lie.
MA. It ain't no lie.
MESSY. You took me in to raise me.
MA. I don't wanna listen to it.

(MESSY grabs MA.)

MESSY. You promised to take care of me.

(MA breaks free.)

MA. You was forced on me. My Pa put you in me. He dragged me down to the river and forced me to take you. He hurt me. You wasn't like Charlie. You brought me pain.

MESSY. I come out of you? You give birth to me? *(She holds out her arms and walks to MA.)* Oh, Mama, please, please hug me.

(MA pushes MESSY to the floor.)

MA. Get away from me.

(MESSY lands by the drawer MA opened earlier while looking for the cure-all. She climbs to her knees and sees the rat poison inside the drawer. She takes the poison and hides it. She climbs to her feet and EXITS.)

MA. Pa was jealous. He come back to run you off. That poor little girl. He didn't think I could find him in a little girls body. But I seen it anyway.

CHARLIE. Messy ain't your pa.

MA. He put her in me right after you was born. And then he grabbed you and tried to drown your little body. He drove me to do what I did. He drove me to kill him. I put him in the river, so his bones would wash away. See, Charlie, that's why I never put you down when you was a baby. I held you in my arms day and night, cause I knew he might come back and try to get you again.

(CHARLIE starts towards the front door.)

CHARLIE. I'm gonna go fetch Messy back.

MA. I'm tryin' to save you. That was a plan. The Devil's plan. He got Anna to come here so she could trick you and try and carry you away. But I ain't gonna let that happen. I fought too hard for you. Now, go get your things, so's we can get goin' from here.

(The front door opens revealing MESSY. She ENTERS with the bottle of cure-all in her hands. She sets it on the table.)

MESSY. Here's what's left of the cure-all. I'm gonna leave now. I know I gotta do this, so things can work out. I'm not gonna be sad, cause I know you really love me.

(MESSY EXITS. MA makes her way to the cure-all. She lifts the bottle to her lips and takes a long sip. She coughs a bit, then looks towards CHARLIE. She takes another long sip and sets the bottle down.)

MA. We gonna be happy now. He knows what's best for you. You understand, don't ya, Charlie? You're all grow'd up now.

(She reaches over and takes another long sip from the bottle. She looks over to CHARLIE and tries to focus on him.)

MA. Ain't you gonna go pack up your stuff?

(He doesn't move. MA starts humming the song she sings when they dance. She moves towards him with her arms stretched out. She's unsteady as the poison MESSY put in the cure-all begins to take effect. She stops to get her balance, then starts moving again. She reaches CHARLIE and holds him around his waist, still humming her song. She touches his face and brushes away his hair. Then collapses in his arms.)

CHARLIE. Ma, what's wrong? *(He lays MA down on th ground and sees MESSY has returned to the doorway.)* Messy, somethin's wrong with Ma.

(MESSY ENTERS.)

MESSY. It's okay, Charlie, I'll take care of her. *(She gives him ANNA'S note.)* Here, Anna give me this note for you. I think she loves you, Charlie. You're lucky to have someone who loves ya. I think she wants to marry you. It's what you're s'pose to do. You ain't s'posed to stay here for the rest of your life. You're s'posed to find yourself a girl. Hurry on, so you don't miss her at the bus.

(CHARLIE runs away after ANNA. MESSY closes the door and walks over to the table and picks up the bottle of cure-all. She lifts the bottle to her lips and takes a long sip. She takes another long sip, then pours the rest out onto the floor. She lays the bottle down and moves over to MA'S body. She kneels down and begins stroking MA'S hair.)

MESSY. I'm sorry I called you the Devil. Cause you're my sweet little girl and I love you most of all.

(She lies down next to MA and puts her head on MA'S chest. She drapes MA'S arm around her and begins singing softly.)

MESSY. "I hear the stars at night. They always make me feel like dancin'."

(Lights fade to black.)

THE END

COSTUME PLOT

MESSY
Scene 1
Skirt and cotton top

Scene 2
Dress
Flats

Act 2
Scene 1
Torn dress
Flats

Scene 2
Panties and cotton top
Skirt and cotton top

Scene 4
Skirt and cotton top
Flats

MA SAMUALS
Scene 1
Dress
Flats

Scene 2
Newer dress
Flats

Act 2
Scene 1
Dress
Flats

Scene 2
Dress
Flats

Scene 4
Dress
Flats

CHARLIE
Scene 1
Overalls
Brown work boots

Scene 2
Same

Act 2
Scene 1
Overalls
Brown work boots
White shirt

Scene 2
Same

Scene 3
Overalls

Scene 4
Overalls
Brown work boots

ANNA
Scene 2
Skirt and blouse
Flats

Act 2
Scene 1
Dress with straps

Scene 2
Same

Scene 3
Same

Scene 4
Same
Flats

PROPERTY PLOT

ONSTAGE
Act 1 &Act 2
Kitchen table, table cloth, and 4 chairs
Rocking chair
Small wood pile
Wood burning stove
Ma's alter
Ma's bible
Picture of Jesus
Candle
Small bottle of holy water
Small porcelain dish filled with religious dust
Religious trinkets
Small cabinet
Chopping block
Knife
Silverware
Dishes
Water glasses
Water pan
Wash basin
Empty cornbread pan
Piece of cornbread on floor
Pecan pie
Bottle of cure-all
Messy's curtained off bedroom
Heavy tattered rope
Fly swatter
Rat poison

OFFSTAGE
Act 1
Messy's broom
Ma's bag of vegetables
Jar of white powder
Rat stick
Charlie's water pail
Wood for stove
Anna's suitcase
Anna's small gift box wrapped with twine
Empty change purse
Charlie's wad of daiseys
Bale of hay
Blanket

OFFSTAGE
Act 2
Messy's pair of earrings
Charlie's white shirt
Two small sticks
Ma's bag of grocery goods
Messy's small bottle of perfume
Charlie's poetry pad
Folded poem in Charlie's pocket

The Clean House
By Sarah Ruhl
2005 Pulitzer Prize Finalist

This extraordinary new play by an exciting new voice in the American drama was runner-up for the Pulitzer Prize. The play takes place in what the author describes as "metaphysical Connecticut", mostly in the home of a married couple who are both doctors. They have hired a housekeeper named Matilde, an aspiring comedian from Brazil who's more interested in coming up with the perfect joke than in house-cleaning. Lane, the lady of the house, has an eccentric sister named Virginia who's just nuts about house-cleaning. She and Matilde become fast friends, and Virginia takes over the cleaning while Matilde works on her jokes. Trouble comes when Lane's husband Charles reveals that he has found his soul mate, or "bashert" in a cancer patient named Anna, on whom he has operated. The actors who play Charles and Anna also play Matilde's parents in a series of dream-like memories, as we learn the story about how they literally killed each other with laughter, giving new meaning to the phrase, "I almost died laughing." This theatrical and wildly funny play is a whimsical and poignant look at class, comedy and the true nature of love. 1m, 4f (#6266)

"Fresh, funny ... a memorable play, imbued with a somehow comforting philosophy: that the messes and disappointments of life are as much a part of its beauty as romantic love and chocolate ice cream, and a perfect punch line can be as sublime as the most wrenchingly lovely aria." — *NY Times*

BARBRA'S WEDDING
Daniel Stern

The Schiffs are the only non-celebrities in their Malibu neighborhood; in fact, their shabby house is next to Barbra Streisand's mansion. As the play opens, Jerry is in a frenzy over the media circus surrounding Barbra's 1998 wedding. An out-of-work actor with one small TV role on his résumé, he resents his obscurity—he wasn't even invited to the wedding! He rages against Streisand, Hollywood, the media, his wife and everything else. His wife tries to leave him—but Schwartzennegger's Humvee is blocking the driveway. This anti-show business comedy by a Hollywood insider is a hilarious send-up with a happy ending. "A ... play in the mold of Elaine May's comedies about people brought near to madness by the quirks of life."—*New York Post.* 1 m., 1 f. (#4901)

DIRTY BLONDE
Claudia Shear
Original score by Bob Stillman

A bawdy New York hit with dream roles, *Dirty Blonde* is "hands down the best new American play of the season....Take off your hats, boys, Mae West is back on Broadway ... in a compact Rolls Royce of a vehicle. This is no evening of mere impersonation.... *Dirty Blonde* is a multi-layered study of the nature of stardom ... [that] finds the enduring substance in the smoke and mirrors of one actress's stardom, allowing Mae West to shock and delight once again."—*The New York Times.* Vocal Score available. 2 m., 1 f. (#6929)

THE BASIC CATALOGUE OF PLAYS AND MUSICALS
online at www.samuelfrench.com